SOLO Wildlife

Elephant

Written and illustrated by David Kennett

SOLOS

For Simone

Southwood Books Limited
4 Southwood Lawn Road
London N6 5SF

First published in Australia by Omnibus Books 2001
This edition published in the UK under licence from
Omnibus Books by
Southwood Books Limited, 2001.

This edition produced for The Book People Ltd.,
Hall Wood Avenue, Haydock, St Helens WA11 9UL

Text and illustrations copyright © David Kennett 2001
Cover design by Lyn Mitchell
Typeset by Clinton Ellicott, Adelaide
Printed in Singapore

ISBN 1 903207 42 8

The elephant

🐘 is a warm-blooded animal

🐘 is the world's largest land mammal

🐘 can remember the call of over 100 other elephants, even when it has not heard them for several years

🐘 looks after other elephants in its herd, and likes to touch and caress its friends.

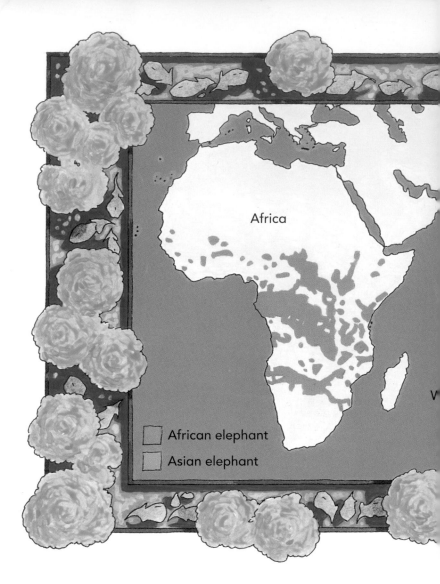

Africa

☐ African elephant
☐ Asian elephant

Once there were millions of elephants
in Africa and Asia. Elephants are
very big animals. They need to
roam over a large area for food
and water.

People need land too, and so elephants now have a smaller area to live in. This map shows where elephants live now.

Elephants are the heaviest and most powerful living animals. They eat plants as their main food. Plant-eating animals are called herbivores.

Here are some other large herbivores.

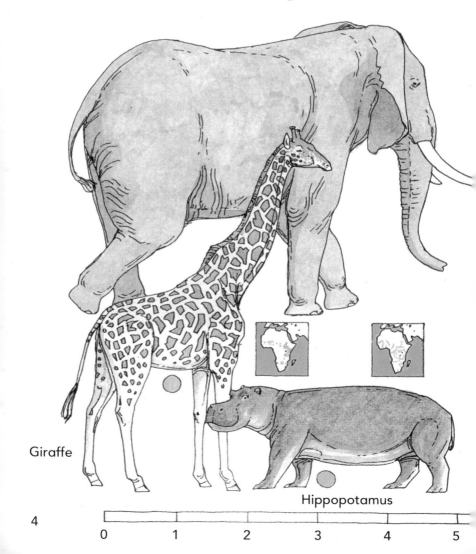

Giraffe

Hippopotamus

0 1 2 3 4 5

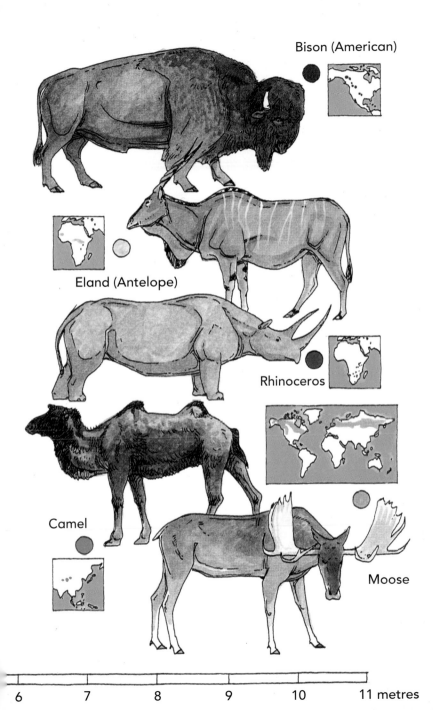

Bison (American)

Eland (Antelope)

Rhinoceros

Camel

Moose

6   7   8   9   10   11 metres

5

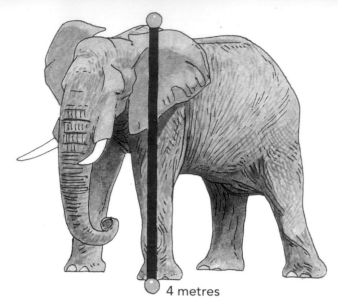

4 metres

This male African elephant measures 4 metres from the top of his shoulder to the ground.

The female African elephant below measures 2.6 metres.

The African elephant has very large ears.

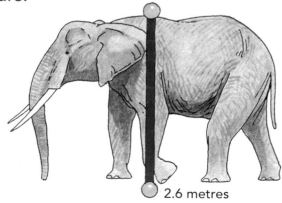

2.6 metres

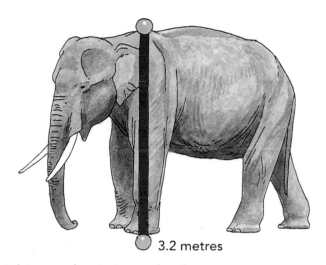

3.2 metres

This male Asian elephant measures 3.2 metres from the top of his shoulder to the ground.

This female Asian elephant measures 2.5 metres. The female Asian elephant does not have tusks. The Asian elephant has smaller ears than the African elephant.

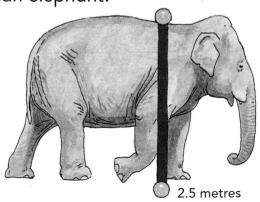

2.5 metres

Asian elephants live in the tropical forest. There is shade to keep them cool.

African elephants live in grassland and open woodland. In Africa, an elephant might have to walk a long way to rest under a shady tree.

This male African elephant weighs 6096 kilograms. A polar bear can weigh 453 kilograms. It would take about 13 and a half polar bears to make up the weight of this elephant.

5.79 metres

By standing on its hind legs and stretching up its trunk an elephant can reach food that is nearly 6 metres above the ground.

Elephants keep growing for most of their lives. The oldest elephants are usually the biggest.

Elephants are old at 60 years, but some can live to 70 or even 80 years old.

Elephants live in small family groups of about 12 animals. A group of elephants is called a herd. There are separate herds for males and for females. The female herd is made up of mothers and their young.

Young elephants are called calves.
Male calves stay with their mothers
until they are old enough to join
a male herd. In the female herd
the oldest and biggest elephant is
the leader.

Small herds often feed and travel together. Elephants in the herd take care of each other. If one of them is sick, other elephants will walk on either side of it and help it to walk.

Elephants of the herd stay with a dying elephant. They will cover a dead elephant with vegetation. Elephants never walk faster than the slowest member of the herd.

Elephants can change how their environment looks. When elephants feed on tree bark the trees can die.

Elephant droppings contain the seeds of bushes and trees. New trees will grow.

Trees and bushes grow back thicker where elephants eat off the small branches.

Elephants dig water holes that help other animals.

When it is thirsty an elephant uses its trunk to suck up water. It puts the tip of its trunk in its mouth and raises its head to make the water flow down its throat.

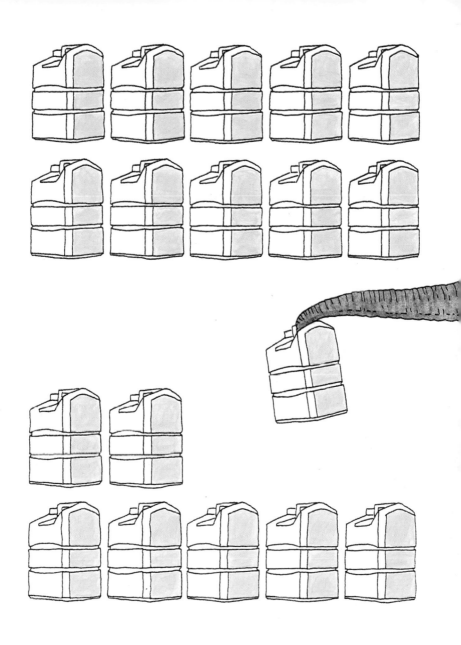

An elephant can drink 180 litres of water every day.

The elephant's skin is thick, grey and wrinkly. It looks tough, but flies and mosquitoes can bite into it. A mud bath cools the elephant's skin. It heals cuts. Mud protects against insect bites.

Mud also stops the sun from drying and cracking the skin. As they get old, some Asian elephants develop pink patches on their faces, trunks, ears and bellies.

Elephants like to have a bath every day and are very good swimmers. They can swim underwater with just their trunks at the surface taking in air.

One elephant from India swam to the islands in the Bay of Bengal and back again. Over the 12 years he took to do the trip, this elephant swam about 321 kilometres.

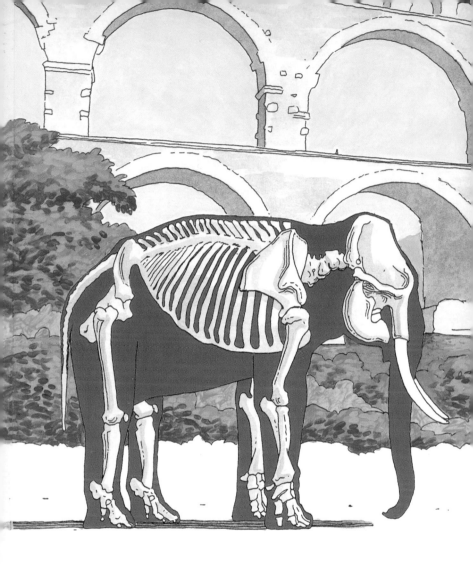

When it is standing at rest, an elephant's legs are straight. Its back bone arches upwards in the middle. Straight legs and an arched back support an elephant's great weight.

Aqueducts, tunnels, roof arches, tables
and chairs all use straight legs and
arches in their design.

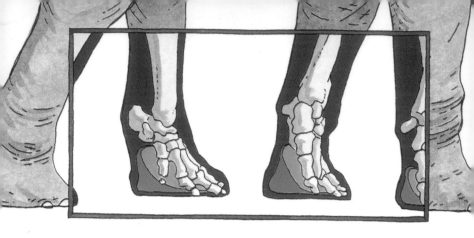

The elephant walks quietly on tiptoe. Its foot is a big, spongy pad of fat and tissue. The weight of the elephant is spread evenly over the foot.

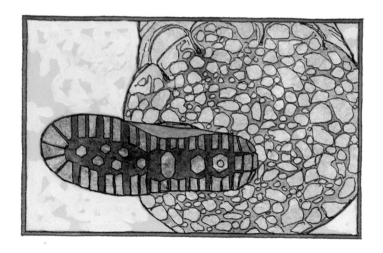

The sole of the elephant's foot has cracks and ridges on it. Like the sole of a hiking boot, the elephant's foot grips well on slippery ground.

Elephants climb up mountain paths without any trouble. They are awkward going down hill. Their tusks, skull and trunk make them front-heavy, and they are in danger of tipping over.

African elephants have big ears.
These can be up to 1.8 metres long
and 1.5 metres wide. The Asian
elephant's smaller ears keep it cool
enough in its shady home in the forest.

1.8 metres

1.5 metres

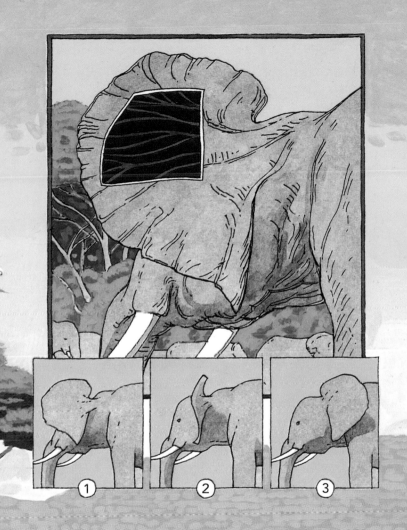

The elephant's ears are a cooling
system. Under the skin there are many
blood vessels. The blood inside is
cooled as the ears are fanned back
and forth.

An elephant's skin looks too big for it. It has many folds and wrinkles. This large area of skin helps the elephant stay cool. The blood cools down near the surface of the skin.

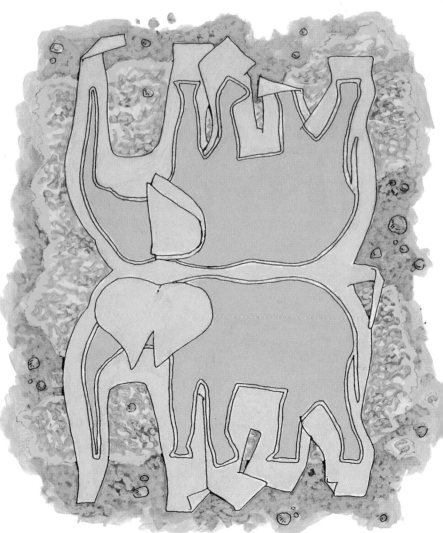

Having a bath or rolling in mud is the best way for elephants to stay cool. The wrinkles in the elephant's skin trap the water and the cool mud.

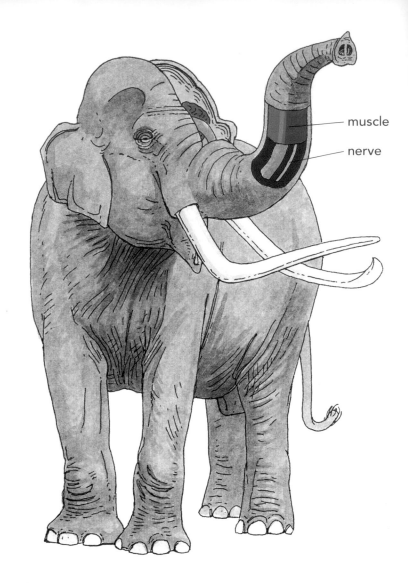

muscle

nerve

The elephant's trunk has thousands
of muscles. An elephant uses its trunk
to pick up food and to suck up water.
It also uses it to pull down branches,
to shift trees or to knock things down.

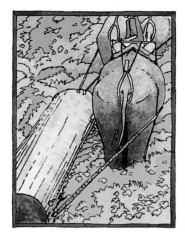 

The elephant has a gentle nature.
It is very intelligent and has a good
memory.

Elephants are easy to work with and to
train. They move logs in forests. They
carry tourists on safari.

African elephant   Asian elephant

At the tip of the elephant's trunk are 'fingers'. The African elephant has two and the Asian elephant has one. These can pick up small, delicate objects or wipe away dirt in the elephant's eye.

At the tip of the trunk are the nostrils.
By raising its trunk and sniffing the air
an elephant can smell food, water and
danger that are too far away to see.

The elephant's tusks are made of ivory.
People have carved ivory for
thousands of years. Many beautiful
objects have been made from ivory.

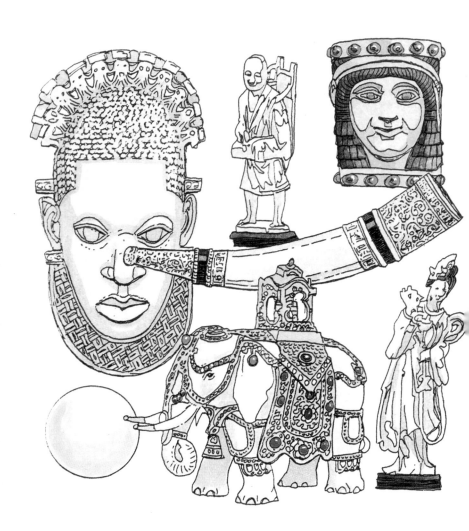

Elephants are killed for their tusks. So many elephants were killed that the sale of ivory was banned.

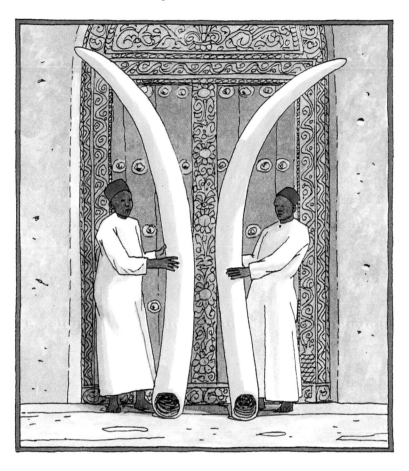

The heaviest tusk recorded weighed 102 kilograms. The longest tusk ever recorded was 3.45 metres long.

Eating plants wears down an elephant's teeth. During its life time an elephant has six sets of molar teeth. When a tooth wears down it is pushed out by a new tooth.

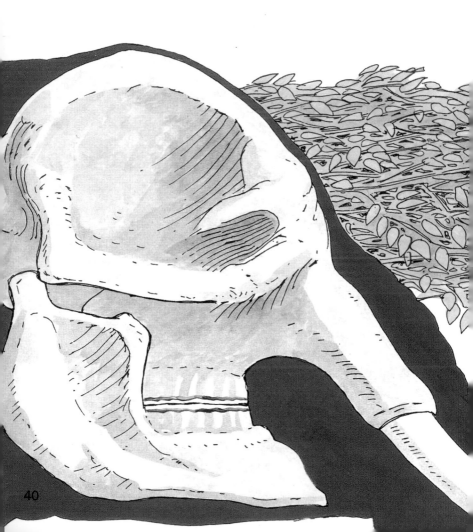

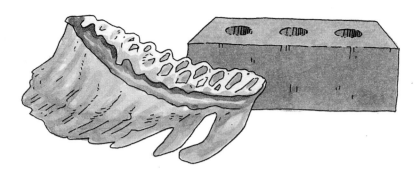

Each new set of molars is bigger than the set before. The elephant's last set of teeth are the size of a house brick. Each tooth weighs around 3 kilograms.

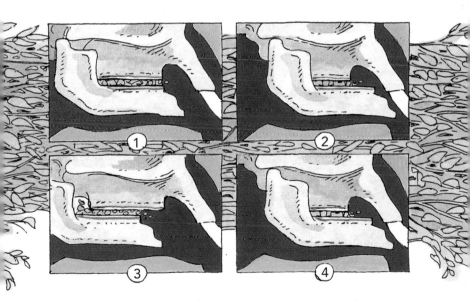

When the elephant chews, its lower jaw moves back and forth. Food is quickly ground down ready to swallow.

Adult male elephants are called bulls. Bull elephants usually live in a herd with other males.

Bull elephants may fight each other for a female.

Adult bulls travel with the female group when one of the females is ready to mate. After mating, the bull elephant returns to the bull herd.

The elephant mother is pregnant for 20 to 22 months. She usually gives birth to one calf. Twins are rare.

Hyenas will try to catch the newborn elephant calf.

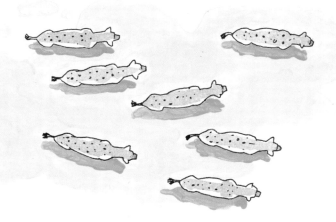

An elephant calf can also be killed by lions.

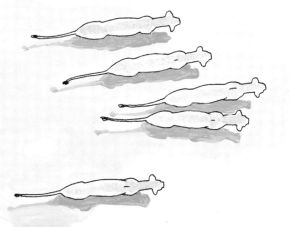

When the mother is about to give birth, other elephants will stay with her. They protect the mother and the calf.

The mother elephant gives birth standing up. It takes only a few minutes. With support from its mother and aunt the calf is standing soon after its birth.

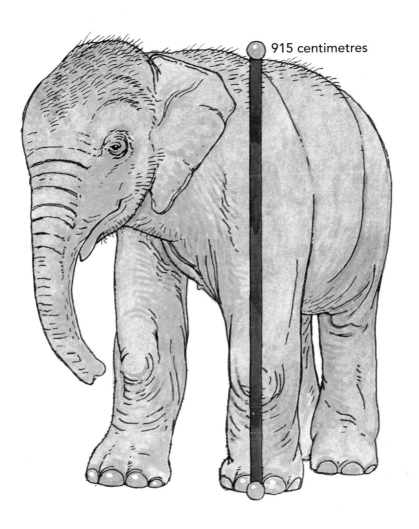

915 centimetres

A newborn elephant weighs more than the average adult human. This calf weighs 100 kilograms. He measures 915 centimetres from the ground to the top of his shoulder.

For the first three to four months of life, baby elephants drink about 12 litres of their mother's milk every day. After three months they start eating plants as well.

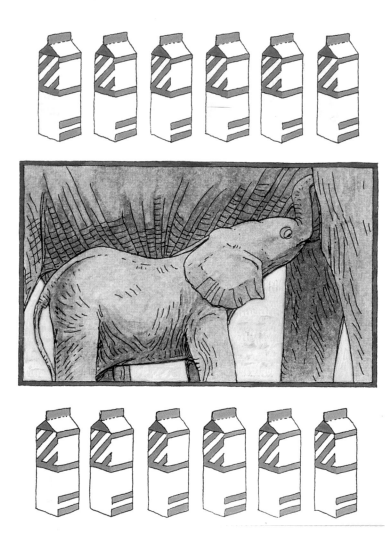

It takes time for the calf to learn how to use its trunk. Sometimes it steps on it by mistake. Calves enjoy their life, playing with each other and chasing birds and small animals.

They love the water and learn to swim very early.

During the hottest part of the afternoon elephants will find some shade to stand under. They might sleep for about four hours standing up.

Late at night elephants will lie down
and sleep deeply for two or three hours.

They often snore.

Hannibal was a general from the north African city of Carthage. He once led an army and many elephants over the mountains and surprised his Roman enemies.

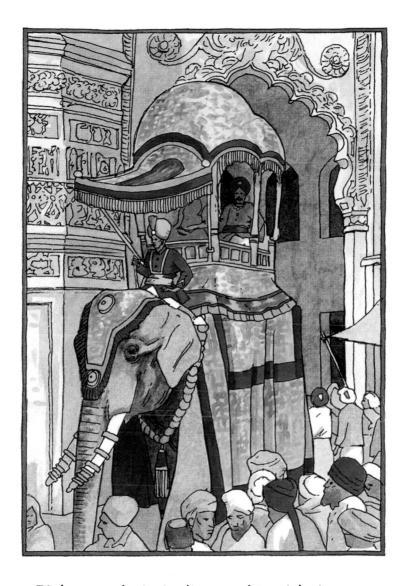

Rich people in India used to ride in a
howdah. This is a richly decorated seat
that the elephant carried on its back.

An Indian folktale tells of a time when
elephants could fly. One day a flock of
elephants landed in a tree. A branch
fell on a man who was sitting under
the tree, thinking. He was cross. He
used his power of thought to take
away the elephant's wings.

The Hindu god of wisdom is called Ganesh. Statues of Ganesh have the head of an elephant and a fat human body with four arms.

When Julius Caesar invaded Britain he knew he would have to fight the warriors who lived there. These were brave and fierce men.

Caesar took an elephant to Britain.
He knew it would scare the Britons.
They would never have seen an animal
like it before.

In Asia, forest land is disappearing.
There are now fewer places where
elephants can live.

Ivory poachers kill elephants in some
parts of Africa.

National parks and reserves in African countries offer some elephants the hope of survival. Money from tourism is very important in keeping some land free for elephants.

Glossary

aqueduct • a bridge that was built to carry water.

environment • an animal's surroundings; the place where it lives.

herbivore • animal that eats plants as its main food.

herd • group of animals.

ivory • the substance that an elephant's tusks are made of.

mammal • animal whose young is fed on milk from the mother's body.

poaching • hunting and killing protected animals for money.

predator • animal that hunts and kills other animals for its food.

prey • animal that is hunted and killed by another animal.

territory • the area of land that an animal hunts in and defends against other animals.

tusk • a kind of long pointed tooth.

vegetation • plants.

warm-blooded animal • an animal whose blood temperature stays at between 36 and 44 degrees Celsius in cold or hot weather. Humans keep their temperature at this level in winter by wearing warm clothes.

Index